14 Short Stories About

DOGS

In Easy English

Jenny Goldmann

BELLANOVA

MELBOURNE · SOFIA · BERLIN

14 Short Stories About Dogs

in Easy English

www.bellanovabooks.com

Copyright © 2026 by Jenny Goldmann

ISBN: 978-619-264-123-8
Imprint: Bellanova Books

All rights reserved. No part of this book may be reproduced in any form by any electronic or mechanical means including photocopying, recording, or information storage and retrieval without permission in writing from the author.

CONTENTS

Introduction	4
Dog Vocabulary	8
A Nose for Clues	10
Sam Goes for Gold	23
The Dog With No Name	34
Paws and the Paranormal	46
Pawsitively Confident	56
Ruffles, The Dog Who Hated Walks	70
The Dog Next Door	82
English on a High Note	96
One Small Step for a Dog	106
The Coolest Dog in Town	119
Woofy's Wonderful Meals	129
Muffle's Marvelous Mustache	139
Unleashing the Past	150
The Dog Who Could See the Future	161

INTRODUCTION

INTRODUCTION

Welcome to "Short Stories about Dogs in Easy English," where you'll find an adorable collection of heartwarming, humorous, and sometimes silly tales about our canine companions. Written in easy English, this book is perfect for English language learners who love dogs and want to improve their reading skills.

We understand that language learning can be difficult, which is why this book is perfect for beginner to intermediate English learners. Even if you find many of the words difficult, don't be put off. Focus on the words you know, and you'll be amazed at how quickly you'll progress!

Why short stories?

Short stories are an excellent way to improve your English language skills. They are designed to be easily digestible, which means you can read them quickly and often, building up your vocabulary and grammar skills over time.

Reading short stories in English can also help you improve your vocabulary, including idiomatic expressions and colloquialisms that are commonly used in everyday conversations.

Additionally, they help you to understand the structure and grammar of the English language in a fun and rewarding way.

INTRODUCTION

How to use this book

To get the most out of this book, we recommend the following tips:

Read regularly: Make a habit of reading in English on a regular basis. This will help you to build up your vocabulary and grammar skills over time.

Take notes: As you read, take notes on new words and phrases that you come across. You can also note down sentence structures and grammar rules that you find difficult to understand.

Practice speaking: Use the new vocabulary and grammar that you have learned in the short stories in your conversations with other English speakers. This will help you to internalize the language and improve your fluency.

Test yourself: Use the quiz at the end of each story to test your knowledge, and use the speaking/writing prompts to challenge yourself even further.

Stay positive: When you read a book in a new language, you might not know every word. That's okay! Don't worry too much about the words you don't know. Instead, try to understand the story using the words you do know. If you don't know a word, you can write it down and look it up later. Reading is supposed to be fun, so don't worry too much if you don't know every word. Just focus on what you understand and enjoy the story.

And finally, don't forget to take breaks to cuddle your own furry friend! Enjoy the stories, and watch your English language skills grow.

DOG VOCABULARY

bark - the sound dogs make
canine - relating to dogs
collar - a band of material worn around a dog's neck for identification, control, or other purposes
fetch - a game where a dog retrieves a thrown object (usually a ball or stick) and returns it to the thrower
leash - a rope or chain used to control and lead a dog
paws - the feet of dogs
snout - the nose and mouth of a dog
treat - food given to dogs as a reward or to reinforce good behavior
woof - another word for bark, the sound dogs make

breed - a type of dog with similar characteristics and traits
digging - the act of using a dog's paws to move or remove dirt
grooming - the act of cleaning and maintaining a dog's coat and appearance
howl - a long, loud sound that dogs make
pack - a group of dogs
whimper - a soft, high-pitched sound that dogs make when they are sad or in pain
litter - a group of puppies born to the same parents

A NOSE FOR CLUES

Max was a smart and loyal golden retriever who lived with his owner, Officer Jack. Officer Jack was a police officer in their neighborhood, and Max was his trusted companion. One day, while Officer Jack was working on a case, Max showed an incredible sense of smell that caught Officer Jack's attention.

"Max, you have an amazing sense of smell! I think we can use it to solve cases. You can be my assistant!" Officer Jack said, patting Max's head.

Max was thrilled to help Officer Jack and started his training to become a police dog. Officer Jack taught him how to recognize

different smells, and Max quickly became an expert.

One day, Officer Jack received a phone call from a woman who had lost her wedding ring. She had searched everywhere, but the ring was nowhere to be found. Officer Jack and Max arrived at the woman's house to investigate. The woman was upset as the ring was very special to her.

"Officer Jack, please find my ring. It's very important to me," the woman said, tears streaming down her face.

"Don't worry, ma'am. We'll do our best to find it," Officer Jack said, comforting her.

Officer Jack asked the woman where she had last seen the ring. She showed him and Max around the house, but they couldn't find anything. Suddenly, Max's nose twitched, and he started sniffing around the couch. He barked happily, and Officer Jack knew that Max had found something.

"Great job, Max! What did you find?" Officer Jack asked, following Max to the couch.

Max barked again and started scratching at

the cushions. Officer Jack lifted the cushion, and there it was, the woman's wedding ring.

"Oh my goodness! How did you do that, Max?" Officer Jack said, amazed.

"He's amazing, isn't he?" the woman said, hugging Max.

After Max had helped Officer Jack find the lost wedding ring, Officer Jack started to take Max with him on his police work. Max was always helpful in solving cases with his incredible sense of smell.

One day, Officer Jack received a call from a farmer who owned a large farm outside the town. The farmer was worried and told Officer Jack that someone had been stealing his animals. The farmer had installed cameras, but the thief always found a way to avoid them.

A NOSE FOR CLUES

Officer Jack decided to take Max with him to the farm. Max was thrilled to be going on another adventure, and he wagged his tail happily as they set off.

When they arrived at the farm, the farmer was waiting for them at the gate. He was a tall man with a worried look on his face.

"Thank you for coming, Officer Jack. I don't know what to do. Every night, someone steals my chickens and sheep. I've installed cameras, but they don't seem to work," the man explained, holding his head in his hands.

"Don't worry, sir. We'll catch whoever is doing this. Max and I will search the farm and see if we can find any clues," Officer Jack reassured him.

As they searched the farm, Max's nose started twitching, and he began barking at a spot near the fence. Officer Jack walked over to the fence and saw that a few wires had been cut.

"Good boy, Max. Looks like we have a clue," Officer Jack said, patting Max's head.

Officer Jack followed the trail of cut wires and found a hidden path leading to a dark forest. He took out his flashlight and carefully made his way into the forest, with Max behind him.

As they walked deeper into the forest, they heard strange noises coming from a nearby bush. Officer Jack and Max stayed very quiet, and they walked slowly towards the bush.

Suddenly, a man jumped out of the bush and tried to run away. Officer Jack chased after him, but the man was too fast. He disappeared into the thick forest.

A NOSE FOR CLUES

Officer Jack and Max searched the area and found a small hut. They walked up to the hut, and Officer Jack knocked on the door. There was no response. He opened the door and saw that the hut was empty.

Just then, Max started barking loudly, and Officer Jack followed him to the back of the hut. There was a trapdoor leading down to a basement. Officer Jack carefully opened the trapdoor and saw a room filled with stolen animals.

After they gave the stolen animals back to the farmer, Officer Jack and Max continued their investigation to find out why the thief had been stealing them.

Officer Jack found the thief's wallet in the basement and discovered that his name was Carl. He decided to visit Carl in jail to ask him why he had been stealing the animals.

"Carl, why did you steal those animals?" Officer Jack asked, looking at Carl through the jail cell.

"I know it's wrong, Officer Jack. But my family loves animals, and they always wanted a farm. We couldn't afford to buy one, so I thought I'd make them one by stealing the animals," Carl explained, looking sad.

Officer Jack couldn't help but feel sorry for Carl. He realized that Carl had stolen the animals for a good cause, to make his family happy.

Officer Jack decided to speak to the farmer about the situation, and they came up with a plan. The farmer agreed to give some of his animals to Carl's family, and in return, Carl would work on the farm to pay for the damages.

A NOSE FOR CLUES

Carl was thrilled with the agreement, and his family was very happy when they received the animals. They all worked together on the farm and became great friends with the farmer.

From that day on, Carl continued to work on the farm and take care of the animals. Officer Jack and Max would often visit the farm to check on them and make sure everything was okay.

The farmer and Carl would always greet them with a smile and offer them fresh eggs and milk from the animals. Officer Jack and Max were happy to have solved the case, and even happier that they had helped Carl's family fulfill their dream of having a farm.

TEST YOURSELF

1. What did Officer Jack find in the basement of the thief's hideout?
a) Stolen watches and jewelry
b) A time machine
c) The stolen animals

2. How did Officer Jack and Max find the thief's hideout?
a) Max followed his nose
b) The thief left a map
c) The farmer gave them a tip

3. What was the name of the thief?
a) Carl
b) Jack
c) Max

4. What was Carl's reason for stealing the animals?
a) To sell them and make money
b) To make his family happy by creating a farm for them
c) To upset the farmer

5. How did Officer Jack and the farmer resolve the situation with Carl?
a) They let him go free
b) They made him pay a large fine
c) They worked out an agreement where Carl would work on the farm to pay for the damages and receive some animals for his family

DISCUSSION -- SPEAK OR WRITE

1. Do you think Officer Jack made the right decision by working out an agreement with Carl to work on the farm? Why or why not?
2. In what ways did this story show the importance of kindness and understanding?
3. Do you think it's good that dogs are used as working animals? Why or why not?

ANSWERS:

1. a) The stolen animals
2. a) Max followed his nose
3. a) Carl
4. b) To make his family happy by creating a farm for them
5. c) They worked out an agreement where Carl would work on the farm to pay for the damages and receive some animals for his family

SAM GOES FOR GOLD

Sam the dog loved his daily walks with his owner, Emily. She would take him to the park, the beach, and sometimes to the pool. Sam loved running around and playing fetch with Emily, but there was one thing that he was absolutely terrified of, and that was water.

Sam would avoid water at all costs, even if it meant not playing fetch by the beach or the pool. Emily noticed this and tried to encourage him to overcome his fear, but Sam just couldn't do it.

One day, while on their daily walk, Sam met another dog named Marley. Marley was a Golden Retriever, and he loved the water.

SAM GOES FOR GOLD

Sam watched in amazement as Marley jumped into the pond, splashed around, and had a great time.

"Hey, buddy, what's up?" Marley asked, panting and wagging his tail.

Sam, looking at Marley with envy, replied, "Nothing much, I just can't seem to get over my fear of the water."

Marley smiled, "Well, that's too bad. Water is so much fun."

Sam looked at Marley, confused, and asked, "Really? It doesn't scare you?"

Marley chuckled, "No, why would it? I love swimming and playing in the water. Do you want me to show you how it's done?"

Sam's ears perked up, "Really? You think you can help me overcome my fear?"

"Of course! Come on, follow me," Marley said, leading Sam to a nearby pond.

Sam was hesitant, but Marley was patient and encouraging. He slowly coaxed Sam into the water, and before he knew it, Sam was paddling around, having a wonderful time.

"I'm doing it! I'm swimming!" Sam exclaimed.

Marley smiled and swam alongside him, "That's great, Sam! I knew you could do it."

From that day on, Sam loved the water. He would jump into puddles, splash in the ocean, and swim in the pool with Emily. Marley would always be by his side, playing with him and teaching him new tricks.

One day, Emily saw an advertisement for the Dog Olympics, and she thought it would be fun to enter Sam. She knew Sam had become a great swimmer, and believed that he could win if he tried.

"Sam, I have a surprise for you," Emily said, rubbing Sam's belly. "We're going to enter you in the Dog Olympics!"

Sam's ears perked up, "Really? You think I'm ready?"

"I know you're ready, Sam," Emily said, smiling. "You've been training so hard, and you've become an amazing swimmer."

Sam was excited, but also nervous. He had never competed in a swimming competition before, and he didn't want to let Emily down.

The day of the competition arrived, and Sam was nervous. He looked around at the other dogs and some of them were much bigger and stronger than him.

Emily whispered in Sam's ear, "You can do this, Sam. Just remember, have fun and do your best."

SAM GOES FOR GOLD

Sam took a deep breath and stepped up to the starting line. The whistle blew, and Sam jumped into the pool, paddling as fast as he could.

The crowd cheered as Sam raced down the pool, passing one dog after another. He could hear Emily and Marley cheering him on from the sidelines.

Sam felt his muscles start to ache, but he kept pushing himself. Finally, he reached the finish line, and the crowd erupted into cheers.

Sam had won the race, and he couldn't believe it. Emily ran up to him, hugging him and telling him how proud she was.

Marley swam over, "Congratulations, Sam! You did it!"

Sam beamed with pride as he received his

medal, and the other dogs congratulated him. He had never felt so happy and accomplished in his life.

From that day on, Sam continued to train hard and compete in swimming competitions. He even started to teach other dogs how to swim and helped them overcome their fear of water, just like Marley had done for him.

Sam had become a champion swimmer and a role model for other dogs. He never forgot the kindness and patience that Marley had shown him, and always made sure to pass it on to others.

As the years went by, Sam grew old, but he never lost his love for swimming. He would still jump into the ocean and paddle around, enjoying the sun and the waves, and never forgetting how far he had come.

TEST YOURSELF

1. What was Sam's biggest fear?
a) Thunderstorms
b) Fireworks
c) Water
d) Loud noises

2. Who did Sam meet that helped him overcome his fear of water?
a) A cat
b) A bird
c) A horse
d) A dog named Marley

3. **What event did Emily enter Sam in after he became a great swimmer?**
a) A talent show
b) A running race
c) A swimming competition
d) A fashion contest

4. **What advice did Emily give Sam before his big race?**
a) Have fun and do your best
b) Don't worry, you'll win for sure
c) Cheat if you have to
d) None of the above

5. **What breed was Marley, the dog who helped Sam overcome his fear of water?**
a) Labrador Retriever
b) Golden Retriever
c) German Shepherd
d) Beagle

DISCUSSION -- SPEAK OR WRITE

1. What do you think helped Sam overcome his fear of water? How important is it to have friends who support and encourage us?

2. What can we learn from Sam's journey to becoming a champion swimmer? How can we apply these lessons in our own lives, especially when faced with challenges or fears?

3. Can you think of any personal experiences where you have faced a fear? How did you do it?

ANSWERS

1. c) Water
2. d) A dog named Max
3. c) A swimming competition
4. a) Have fun and do your best
5. b) Golden Retriever

THE DOG WITH NO NAME

Once upon a time, in a busy city in California, there was a street dog with no name. He roamed the streets day and night, looking for food and sleeping under old cars or in alleyways. Nobody knew where he came from or who he belonged to, and nobody seemed to care.

But the street dog was a clever one. He had learned to avoid the dangers of the city, like the speeding cars and the cruel kids who threw stones at him. He had also learned to be friendly to the kind-hearted people, who sometimes offered him a scrap of food or a gentle pat on the head.

One day, the street dog was wandering through the city when he came across a beautiful building. It was grander than any

building he had ever seen before, with huge columns and bright windows that sparkled in the sunlight. The street dog was curious and decided to investigate.

He walked through the front gates and into the courtyard, where he saw a group of people in fancy clothes, sipping champagne and nibbling on tiny canapés. The street dog's nose twitched at the delicious smells, and he couldn't resist the temptation to go closer.

As he hid under a table, he overheard the conversation of the guests. They were all talking about the owner of the building, a wealthy and powerful man named Mr. Wilkins.

"Did you hear about his latest purchase?" said one woman. "He just bought a rare diamond the size of a golf ball!"

"He must be the richest man in the world," said a man with a mustache. "I hear he has more money than he knows what to do with."

The street dog listened intently, fascinated by the conversations about riches and wealth. He had never had much himself, and the idea of having more than enough was hard to understand.

Just then, a small boy saw the street dog under the table. He was excited and reached out to pet the dog, but his mother scolded him and pushed the dog away.

The street dog slowly walked away, feeling rejected. He realized that he was just a street dog with no name, and that nobody wanted him around. He lay down under a tree in the courtyard and closed his eyes, dreaming of a life where he could have everything he ever wanted.

The next day, the street dog woke up to the sound of construction. He opened his eyes to see a team of workers building a giant wall around the building he had visited the day before. The street dog watched in confusion as the wall grew taller and taller, until he was

THE DOG WITH NO NAME

completely surrounded by it.

Days turned into weeks, and the street dog was trapped inside the wall. He had no food or water, and nobody came to check on him. He was completely alone, with nothing but his own thoughts to keep him company.

But the street dog was a clever one, and he refused to give up. He spent his days digging through the dirt and looking for scraps of food that had been left behind by the workers. He drank rainwater that collected in puddles and tried to stay positive by imagining a happy future.

One day, as he was digging through the dirt, the street dog hit something hard. He dug deeper, and his paws touched something smooth and cool. He sniffed at it and realized that it was a diamond, just like the one he had heard the guests talking about.

The street dog's heart was filled with excitement. He had heard that diamonds were worth a lot of money, and he knew that if he could get this one out of the wall, he would be richer than he could imagine.

Over the next few days, the street dog worked tirelessly to dig out the diamond. Finally, just as he was about to give up, the street dog managed to pull the diamond out of the wall. It was beautiful and sparkled in the sunlight. The street dog could hardly believe his luck, he had found a diamond!

But then he realized that he had no idea what to do with it. He was just a street dog with no name, he didn't know anything about selling diamonds or making money.

As he sat there, pondering his situation, he heard a voice behind him. "Well, well, well, what do we have here?"

THE DOG WITH NO NAME

It was a scruffy-looking man with a sneaky smile and a glint in his eye. "Looks like you've found yourself a little treasure, haven't you?"

The street dog barked and growled, trying to defend his precious diamond. But the man just laughed and lunged forward, grabbing the diamond out of the street dog's paw.

The street dog was heartbroken. He had worked so hard to find that diamond, only to have it stolen away by a thief. He walked away, feeling more alone and helpless than ever before.

Days turned into weeks, and the street dog continued to wander the streets, trying to survive.

One day, as he was walking along a particularly dirty street, he saw a small girl sitting on a bench, crying. He went closer.

The little girl looked up at him with tears in her eyes. "I lost my puppy," she said. "He ran away, and I can't find him anywhere."

The street dog nudged her gently with his nose, trying to comfort her. He knew what it was like to be lost and alone, and he didn't want this little girl to feel the same way.

The girl looked at the street dog with a mixture of fear and hope. "Can you help me find him?" she asked.

The street dog barked, as if to say, "Of course!"

And so the street dog set out to find the girl's lost puppy. He sniffed and searched and followed his nose, until finally, he caught a whiff of something familiar. It was the scent of another dog, and it was coming from a nearby alleyway.

THE DOG WITH NO NAME

The street dog led the little girl to the alleyway, where they found a scruffy-looking puppy, wagging its tail and barking happily. The little girl scooped up the puppy, tears streaming down her face as she hugged him tight.

"Thank you, thank you!" she cried, as the street dog looked on, feeling a sense of satisfaction that he had never felt before.

From that day on, the street dog was no longer a dog with no name. The little girl had named him Buddy, and she took him home with her, where he was fed and loved and treated like a real member of the family.

And though Buddy never forgot his days as a street dog, he knew that he had found something even more precious than diamonds - a home, a family, and a name.

TEST YOURSELF

1. Where did the street dog live?
a) London
b) California
c) New York City

2. Where was the street dog trapped?
a) Inside a wall
b) Inside a house
c) Up a tree

3. What was the street dog digging for?
a) A box of money
a) A bone
a) A diamond

4. **Who was Mr. Wilkins?**
a) One of the richest men in the world
b) A guest at the party
c) The street dog's owner

5. **What name did the girl give to the street dog?**
a) Noah
b) Samuel
c) Buddy

DISCUSSION -- SPEAK OR WRITE

1. What do you think the moral of the story is?
2. Have you ever adopted a dog or another animal from a shelter?
3. What was your favorite part of the story? Why?

ANSWERS

1. b) California
2. a) Inside a wall
3. c) A diamond
4. a) One of the richest men in the world
5. c) Buddy

PAWS AND THE PARANORMAL

One sunny afternoon, Reggie, Bella, Duke, and Rosie were lazing in the park when Reggie said, "Hey, have you guys heard about the haunted house on the edge of town?"

Bella raised her ears, "What haunted house?"

Duke barked, "The one that's been abandoned for years."

Rosie looked hesitant, "I don't know, guys. It sounds pretty spooky."

Reggie chuckled, "Come on, Rosie, don't be such a scaredy-dog. Let's go check it out!"

The other dogs agreed, and they set off towards the haunted house. As they approached the house, they could feel the hairs on their backs standing up.

"Are you sure we should be doing this?" Rosie whimpered.

Reggie nudged her, "Don't worry, we're tough dogs. We can handle anything."

Bella rolled her eyes, "Come on, let's go already."

With a bark of excitement, the four dogs entered the haunted house, unaware of the adventure and danger that lay ahead.

As they entered the house, the dogs could feel a cold breeze blowing through the rooms, and the sound of creaking floorboards echoed in the long, spooky hallways. The abandoned house was in a terrible state, with wallpaper peeling off and broken furniture lying around.

Duke sniffed around, trying to catch any scent of danger. "This place gives me the creeps," he said, shuddering.

"You're not the only one. I think we should be

careful and stick together," Bella replied.

As they moved through the house, they could hear strange noises, footsteps, and whispers that made their hair stand on end. The dogs barked loudly, hoping to scare away any ghosts that might be hiding in the shadows.

Suddenly, the door slammed shut, and the dogs were trapped inside. They howled and barked, trying to escape, but all the doors and windows were locked tight.

Rosie began to panic, "Oh no, what are we going to do now? We're trapped!"

Reggie tried to stay calm, "Don't worry, guys, we'll find a way out. Let's keep searching the house for clues."

The dogs searched the house, trying to find a way out, but all their efforts were in vain.

They found themselves in a large room with a fireplace, and as they looked around, they saw a young girl floating in the air, smiling at them.

The girl said, "Hello, my name is Amanda. I'm not here to scare you. I'm a friendly ghost who likes to haunt this house and play tricks on visitors."

The dogs were surprised but not scared. They realized that Amanda was just a friendly ghost who wanted to play. They decided to join in and have some fun with her.

Amanda showed them some cool tricks, like floating in the air and making objects move with her mind. The dogs barked and chased after her, having the time of their lives.

As they played, Amanda told them stories about her life as a young girl and how much she loved playing with her dog, who had passed away. She said she missed having a dog to play with and wished she could have a new friend.

The dogs were touched by Amanda's story and realized that they could be her new friends. They invited her to come and play with them anytime she wanted and promised to always be there for her.

From that day on, the dogs visited the haunted house regularly to play with Amanda and have fun. They had made a new friend and learned that sometimes, things that seem scary can turn out to be fun and exciting.

TEST YOURSELF

1. What was the first reaction of the dogs when they saw Amanda?
a) They were scared and wanted to leave
b) They were curious and wanted to learn more about her
c) They were surprised but not scared

2. What did Amanda tell the dogs about her life?
a) She had been trapped in the house for a long time
b) She used to have a dog
c) She hated being a ghost

3. What did the dogs promise Amanda?
a) To leave the haunted house and never come back
b) To always be there for her and play with her anytime she wanted
c) To find a new home for her

4. What did the dogs learn from their experience with Amanda?
a) That ghosts are scary and should be avoided
b) That sometimes, things that seem scary can turn out to be fun and exciting
c) That haunted houses are dangerous and should not be visited

5. What was the outcome of the dogs' adventure in the haunted house?
a) They made a new friend and learned an important lesson about fear
b) They failed to find a way out and remained trapped
c) They uncovered a dark secret and helped solve a mystery

DISCUSSION -- SPEAK OR WRITE

1. Would you have been scared of Amanda, or would you want to play with her like the dogs did?
2. What lessons did the dogs learn about friendship, kindness, and overcoming fear?
3. Have you ever been scared of something that turned out to be fun and exciting? How did you feel when you realized that it wasn't as scary as you thought? What did you learn from that experience?

Answers

1. c) They were surprised but not scared
2. b) She used to have a dog
3. b) To always be there for her and play with her anytime she wanted
4. b) That sometimes, things that seem scary can turn out to be fun and exciting
5. a) They made a new friend and learned an important lesson about fear

PAWSITIVELY CONFIDENT

Once upon a time, in a small village nestled in the rolling hills of the countryside, there lived a little girl named Ella. She was a shy and timid child, and often found it difficult to make friends. She longed for someone to talk to, play with, and share her adventures with.

One sunny day, Ella was exploring the fields when she heard a strange noise. She looked around and saw a scruffy-looking dog with a wagging tail and a friendly smile. The dog, whose name was Buster, barked and ran towards her. Ella was a little scared at first, but she soon realized that Buster was harmless and just wanted to play.

"Hello there, little pup. What are you doing all

alone out here?" Ella asked the dog.

Buster wagged his tail and licked her hand. Ella smiled and scratched him behind his ears.

"You're a friendly one, aren't you? Do you want to be friends?" Ella asked.

Buster barked and jumped up, as if to say "yes".

From that day on, Ella and Buster became best friends. They went on long walks through the countryside, played fetch in the fields, and cuddled up together under the shade of a tree. Ella felt happier than she had in a long time, and she knew that Buster was the reason for it.

One day, as they were playing in the park, Ella saw a group of children playing on the

PAWSITIVELY CONFIDENT

swings. She really wanted to join in, but she was too shy to talk to them. Buster, however, had other ideas.

"Come on, Ella! Let's go say hi to those kids over there!" Buster barked.

Ella hesitated, but she trusted Buster. She followed him as he bounded over to the group of children, barking and wagging his tail.

"Hey there, guys! My name is Buster. What's yours?" Buster said.

The children were a little startled at first, but they soon realized that Buster was harmless and just wanted to play. They introduced themselves to him, and soon they were all playing together.

Ella watched from a distance, too shy to join in. But when she saw how much fun the children were having with Buster, she knew she wanted to be a part of it.

"Hi, my name is Ella. Can I play with you guys?" Ella asked nervously.

"Of course you can! We're having so much fun with Buster, and we would love for you to join us!" one of the children said.

Ella smiled and walked over to them. Buster wagged his tail happily as she joined in the game.

As the sun began to set, the children had to go home. Ella and Buster said goodbye, and as they walked back to their house, Ella couldn't stop talking about how much fun she had.

"Did you see that, Buster? I made new friends! Thank you so much for helping me," Ella said.

Buster wagged his tail, as if to say you're welcome.

Over the next few weeks, Ella continued to

play with Buster and her new friends. They went on adventures through the fields, built forts in the woods, and had picnics by the river.

Ella's parents were thrilled to see their daughter so happy and outgoing. They had been worried about her shyness, but Buster had brought her out of her shell and helped her make new friends.

One day, Ella's mom asked her about Buster.

"Where did you find that friendly dog, Ella?" her mom asked.

"I found him in the fields a few weeks ago. He's my best friend now!" Ella said.

"Well, he's a great dog. I think he's been a good influence on you," her mom said.

Ella smiled. "He really has. I used to be so shy and scared, but now I feel like I can do anything with Buster by my side."

Buster barked happily and licked Ella's hand, as if to say he agreed.

As the weeks turned into months, Ella's confidence continued to grow. She no longer felt afraid to approach new people or try new things. Buster had shown her that anything was possible with a little courage and a good friend by your side.

One day, Ella and her friends decided to have a big picnic in the park. They brought blankets, sandwiches, and a ball to play with. Buster came along too, of course.

As they were eating their sandwiches, Ella noticed a shy boy sitting alone on a bench nearby. He looked sad and lonely, and Ella knew exactly how he felt.

"Hey guys, do you see that boy over there? He looks like he could use a friend," Ella said.

Her friends looked over and agreed. They walked over to the boy and introduced themselves. At first, he was hesitant, but they soon made him feel welcome.

Buster barked happily and licked the boy's hand, as if to say welcome to the group.

"Thanks for inviting me over. I'm usually pretty shy, but you guys seem really nice," the boy said.

Ella smiled. "We know how you feel. But with us and Buster here, you'll never be alone."

The boy smiled back, and soon they were all playing together, laughing and having a great time.

As the sun began to set, and it was time to go home, Ella felt a sense of happiness and pride. She had not only made new friends but helped someone else who was shy and lonely, just like she used to be.

"Thanks for inviting me to this picnic. I had a great time," the boy said.

"We're so glad you came. You're welcome to join us anytime," Ella said.

Buster barked happily and licked the boy's hand, as if to say see you again soon.

As Ella and her friends walked home, she knew that she had found a true friend in Buster. He had not only helped her make new friends but had shown her the power of kindness and inclusion.

"I'm so lucky to have you, Buster. You're the

best friend anyone could ever ask for," Ella said.

From that day on, Ella and Buster continued to have many more adventures together. They explored the countryside, went on treasure hunts, and made even more friends along the way. And through it all, Ella knew that she had a loyal and trustworthy friend in Buster, who had helped her overcome her shyness and taught her the true meaning of friendship.

TEST YOURSELF

1. What is the name of the dog that becomes Ella's best friend?
a) Sparky
b) Buster
c) Spot

2. How does Ella feel about making new friends at the beginning of the story?
a) Excited
b) Confident
c) Shy

3. What activity do Ella and her new friends do together during their picnic?
a) Build forts in the woods
b) Go on treasure hunts
c) Play with a ball
d) All of the above

4. How does Ella feel after making new friends and helping the shy boy?
a) Happy and proud
b) Scared and nervous
c) Angry and frustrated
d) Indifferent and uninterested

5. What lesson does Ella learn from her friendship with Buster?
a) The power of kindness and inclusion
b) The importance of being selfish
c) The value of being shy and timid
d) None of the above

DISCUSSION -- SPEAK OR WRITE

1. What do you think Ella learned from her dog friend Buster? How did Buster help her make new friends even though she was shy?
2. Have you ever felt shy or found it hard to make new friends? How did you deal with it?
3. In the story, Ella and her friends made a new boy feel welcome. Have you ever made someone feel welcome? How did it feel?

Answers

1. b) Buster
2. c) Shy
3. d) All of the above
4. a) Happy and proud
5. a) The power of kindness and inclusion

RUFFLES, THE DOG WHO HATED WALKS

Ruffles lived in a small village in a beautiful house surrounded by fields. However, Ruffles was a lazy dog who hated going for walks. His owners, Mr. and Mrs. Johnson, loved taking long strolls through the village with Ruffles, but he always made a fuss.

Every time they took him out, Ruffles would lie down on the ground and refuse to move. Mr. and Mrs. Johnson would have to coax him out with treats and pull on his leash to get him to move.

One day, Mr. Johnson decided that enough was enough. He was tired of Ruffles' behavior, and he wanted to teach him a lesson. So, he

came up with a plan.

The next morning, Mr. Johnson woke up early and prepared for his walk. He put on his walking shoes, grabbed his hat, and whistled for Ruffles to come outside. Ruffles groaned and dragged himself out of bed.

When Ruffles saw that Mr. Johnson was dressed for a walk, he immediately lay down on the ground and refused to move. But Mr. Johnson was ready for him. He took out a large piece of steak from the fridge and held it up in front of Ruffles' nose.

"Come on, boy. Let's go for a walk. You can have this steak when we get back."

Ruffles' eyes widened at the sight of the steak. He loved steak more than anything in the world. He got up and wagged his tail, excited to go for a walk.

They walked through the village, and Ruffles was having a great time. He sniffed everything in sight and chased after birds. Mr. Johnson was pleased to see that Ruffles was finally enjoying himself.

After a while, they came to a fork in the road.

One path led to the left, and the other to the right. Mr. Johnson wanted to take the right path, but Ruffles tugged on his leash and pulled him to the left.

Mr. Johnson was confused. He had never seen Ruffles act like this before. Ruffles usually just followed him wherever he went.

"Come on, boy. Let's go this way," Mr. Johnson said, tugging on Ruffles' leash.

But Ruffles refused to move. He sat down on the ground and looked up at Mr. Johnson with his beautiful big eyes.

Mr. Johnson was starting to get annoyed. He didn't understand why Ruffles was acting this way. He decided to try a different tactic.

"Okay, Ruffles. You win. We'll go your way," Mr. Johnson said.

Ruffles jumped up and wagged his tail, excited that he had won. They walked down the left path, and Ruffles led the way.

After a few minutes, they came to a dark, spooky forest. Mr. Johnson didn't like the look of it, but Ruffles was eager to explore. He pulled Mr. Johnson into the forest, and they walked deeper and deeper into the woods.

They walked for a while longer until they came to a clearing in the forest. In the center of the clearing was a small pond, and on the other side of the pond was a large, beautiful tree.

Ruffles ran towards the tree, and Mr. Johnson followed him. As they got closer, Mr. Johnson noticed that the tree had something strange about it. It was covered in glittering jewels and shimmering gold.

Mr. Johnson couldn't believe his eyes. He

had stumbled upon a treasure trove, and it was all thanks to Ruffles.

Ruffles ran up to the tree and began pawing at the jewels. Mr. Johnson could see that Ruffles was excited, but he was also hesitant.

"Come on, Ruffles. You did all the hard work. You should have the first pick," Mr. Johnson said.

Ruffles wagged his tail and barked happily. He dove into the pile of jewels and gold and began picking out the shiniest and prettiest ones.

Mr. Johnson laughed and watched as Ruffles filled his mouth with as many jewels as he could carry.

Ruffles was overjoyed with his newfound treasure, and Mr. Johnson couldn't believe his luck. As they made their way back home, Mr. Johnson couldn't help but think about how wrong he had been about Ruffles. He had always thought of him as a lazy dog who didn't enjoy going for walks. But today, Ruffles had proved him wrong. He had led them to a treasure trove that they never would have found without him.

From that day on, Mr. Johnson treated Ruffles differently. He no longer saw him as a lazy dog, but as a smart and adventurous companion. They went on many more walks together, and Ruffles always seemed to lead them on exciting adventures.

As for the jewels, Mr. Johnson and his wife decided to sell them and use the money to make improvements to their village. They donated some of the money to the local school and used the rest to build a new park for children to play in.

And Ruffles? Well, he got to keep a few of the jewels as a reward for his bravery and adventurous spirit. From that day on, he was a different dog. He no longer lay down on the ground and refused to move. He was excited to go on walks, and he always led Mr. and Mrs. Johnson on exciting adventures. And, of course, he got to eat his steak.

TEST YOURSELF

1. Why was Mr. Johnson annoyed with Ruffles?
a) Because Ruffles barked too much
b) Because Ruffles was too playful
c) Because Ruffles was lazy and refused to go for walks
d) Because Ruffles chewed on furniture

2. What did Mr. Johnson use to coax Ruffles into going for a walk?
a) A toy
b) A leash
c) A steak
d) A ball

3. What did Ruffles find in the forest?
a) A treasure trove
b) A bird's nest
c) A rabbit hole
d) A stream

4. What did Mr. Johnson and his wife do with the jewels they found?
a) Kept them all for themselves
b) Gave them all to Ruffles as a reward
c) Sold them and donated the money to their village
d) Buried them in the forest for safekeeping

5. How did Ruffles change after finding the treasure?
a) He became more lazy
b) He became more aggressive
c) He became more adventurous
d) He became more obedient

DISCUSSION -- SPEAK OR WRITE

1. Have you ever found something unexpected while on a walk or while exploring? What did you find?

2. Ruffles was initially a lazy dog, but he changed after his adventure in the forest. Have you ever tried something new and surprised yourself with how much you enjoyed it?

3. Mr. Johnson and his wife sold the jewels they found and used the money to make their village a better place. What are some things you could do to make your community a better place?

Answers

1. c) Because Ruffles was lazy and refused to go for walks
2. c) A treat
3. a) A treasure trove
4. c) Sold them and donated the money to their village
5. c) He became more adventurous

THE DOG NEXT DOOR

Once upon a time, in a small town, there lived a little black dog named Baxter. He was a friendly and playful dog, but he was always a bit lonely. His owners, Mr. and Mrs. Brown, were busy working all day, leaving Baxter alone at home.

One day, a new family moved in next door, and with them came a little white dog named Bella. Baxter thought she was the most beautiful dog he had ever seen. He couldn't stop staring at her cute button nose and shiny, white fur.

Baxter started to develop feelings for Bella, and he would bark at her all day, hoping she

would notice him. Bella was shy and would only bark back when she felt comfortable, but she really liked Baxter too.

Baxter was determined to get closer to Bella. He tried to dig a tunnel under the fence, but it was too hard. He tried to sneak out of his garden, but Mr. Brown always caught him.

THE DOG NEXT DOOR

One day, Baxter noticed that Bella's owners were going away for the weekend. He saw this as an opportunity to finally spend some time with Bella.

He waited until Mr. and Mrs. Brown were asleep, then snuck out of his garden and went to Bella's garden. Bella was waiting for him, and they ran and played all night long.

As the sun was starting to rise, Baxter and Bella cuddled up under a tree. Suddenly, they heard a loud noise. It was a group of dogs, and they didn't look friendly.

Baxter and Bella were scared. They tried to run, but the other dogs were too fast. They were surrounded.

One of the dogs stepped forward. "What are you doing in our territory?" he growled.

"We didn't mean to intrude," Baxter said. "We were just playing."

The other dogs didn't believe them. They started to circle around Baxter and Bella, getting closer and closer.

Baxter had to think fast. He knew he had to protect Bella.

He barked as loud as he could, and the other dogs stopped for a moment. Baxter took this opportunity to run towards the fence. Bella followed him.

The other dogs were getting closer, but Baxter and Bella were too fast. They managed to crawl under the fence and back into their gardens.

They were both shaking. Baxter had never been so scared in his life. But he was also proud. He had protected Bella, and he had proven to himself that he was brave.

As the days went by, Baxter and Bella's friendship grew stronger. They would bark at each other through the fence, and Baxter would tell Bella about his day.

One day, Baxter noticed that Bella was not in her garden. He barked and barked, but she didn't answer.

Baxter started to worry. What if something had happened to Bella?

He decided to take a risk and go to her garden. When he arrived, he saw that Bella was not alone. There was another dog with her, a big, scary dog that Baxter had never seen before.

Baxter was scared, but he knew he had to

protect Bella. He ran towards the big dog, barking as loud as he could.

The big dog was surprised and backed off. Bella ran over to Baxter and hugged him.

"Thank you for saving me, Baxter," she said. "That was Boris from the other neighborhood. He's not very friendly."

Baxter was proud that he had saved Bella again.

But suddenly, they heard a loud voice. It was Mr. Brown.

"Baxter, come back here," he shouted. "You're not allowed to go over there."

Baxter knew he had to go back to his garden, but he didn't want to leave Bella.

"Don't worry," Bella said. "I'll see you soon!"

Baxter nodded and ran back to his garden. He missed Bella terribly and wished they could be together all the time.

The next day, Baxter decided to talk to Mr. Brown. "Please, can I see Bella?" he asked.

Mr. Brown thought for a moment. "Okay, but you have to be careful. I don't want you to get hurt."

Baxter was overjoyed. He couldn't wait to see Bella again.

The next day, Baxter and Bella decided to go on an adventure. They ran through the town, exploring every corner and chasing squirrels.

They went through a park where they found a little puppy who was lost and scared.

"We have to help him," Bella said.

Baxter nodded. "Let's bark at him and get his attention."

They barked and barked until the puppy followed them back to Bella's garden. They gave him food and water and waited for his owners to come pick him up.

But as they were waiting, they heard a loud noise. It was the same group of dogs that had chased them before. They had followed them and were now at Bella's garden, ready to attack.

Baxter and Bella knew they had to act fast. They couldn't let the other dogs hurt the puppy.

Baxter barked as loud as he could, and Bella ran towards the fence. She started to dig a hole under it. Baxter joined her, and they dug as fast as they could.

The other dogs were getting closer and closer, but Baxter and Bella were determined. They finally managed to dig a big enough hole for the puppy to crawl under the fence.

The other dogs were surprised, but they didn't give up. They tried to crawl under the fence too, but they were too big.

Baxter and Bella had saved the puppy. They felt proud and happy.

From that day on, Baxter and Bella were known as the heroes of the town. Everyone knew their story, and everyone admired their friendship.

Mr. and Mrs. Brown realized that true love knows no boundaries, and they learned to appreciate the special bond between Baxter and Bella. They allowed the dogs to spend as much time together as they wanted, knowing that their love was pure and unconditional.

In the end, Baxter and Bella lived happily ever after, always barking and playing with each other through the fence that separated their gardens. They knew that no matter what, they would always be there for each other.

TEST YOURSELF

1. What did Baxter do to try and get closer to Bella?
a) Dig a tunnel under the fence
b) Climb over the fence
c) Write a love letter to Bella's owners

2. What did Baxter and Bella find in the park?
a) A group of friendly dogs
b) A lost and scared puppy
c) A big pile of treats

3. What did Baxter and Bella do when they were surrounded by the other dogs?
a) They fought the other dogs
b) They barked as loud as they could and ran towards the fence
c) They pretended to be dead

4. How did Baxter and Bella save the lost puppy?
a) They barked at the puppy until it followed them back to Bella's garden
b) They chased the puppy until it ran towards the fenc
c) They dug a hole under the fence so the puppy could crawl back to safety

5. What did Mr. and Mrs. Brown learn about true love?
a) True love should be kept apart by fences
b) True love knows no boundaries
c) True love is only for humans, not dogs

DISCUSSION -- SPEAK OR WRITE

1. Have you ever had a friend you couldn't see all the time? How did you feel about it? What did you do to stay in touch?
2. Baxter and Bella were very brave when they were surrounded by the other dogs. Do you think you would have been brave like them? What would you have done in that situation?
3. Baxter and Bella learned that true love knows no boundaries. What do you think that means?

Answers

1. a) Dig a tunnel under the fence
2. b) A lost and scared puppy
3. b) They barked as loud as they could and ran towards the fence
4. c) They dug a hole under the fence so the puppy could crawl back to safety
5. b) True love knows no boundaries

ENGLISH ON A HIGH NOTE: LOLA AND BRUNO'S LONDON ADVENTURE

Bruno and Lola were two Spanish dogs living in Madrid. They were bored of just barking in Spanish all day long, and they wanted to learn a new language. They decided to learn English so that they could speak to people from all over the world, and they had heard that London was the best place to learn it. So, they packed their bags and headed to London.

As soon as they arrived, they started their language-learning adventure. They met a friendly squirrel in the park who told them about an English class for dogs. The class

was held every day in a park near their home.

The first day of class was exciting. Bruno and Lola arrived early, eager to learn. But as soon as the class began, they realized that it was going to be difficult. The teacher was talking very fast, and the other dogs in the class seemed to know more than they did.

Bruno looked at Lola and whispered, "I don't understand anything that the teacher is saying. This is going to be hard."

Lola whispered back, "Don't worry, we'll find a way to learn."

And that's exactly what they did. Instead of sitting in class, they started exploring the city. They visited museums, parks, and shops. Everywhere they went, they listened carefully to people speaking English. They even made friends with some humans who taught them new words every day.

One day, they met a friendly parrot in the park. The parrot noticed that Bruno and Lola were struggling to learn English and offered to help.

The parrot said, "I learned English by singing songs. Maybe that will help you too."

Bruno and Lola looked at each other and then back at the parrot. They had never heard of such a thing, but they were willing to try.

So, the parrot taught them a song called "The Wheels on the Bus." Bruno and Lola sang the song over and over again until they knew it by heart.

The next day, they went to the park and sang the song to the other dogs. The other dogs were impressed and asked how they had learned the song so quickly.

Bruno and Lola explained their unique method of learning, and soon all the dogs in the class were singing "The Wheels on the Bus."

But Bruno and Lola didn't stop there. They continued to explore the city and find new ways to learn. They went to a play where they watched humans acting out scenes in English. They watched movies with subtitles, and they even learned to read English books.

One day, they met a human who was studying Spanish. The human was struggling to learn, just like Bruno and Lola had been. So, they taught the human some Spanish words, while the human taught them some English words.

They soon became good friends and would meet up every day to practice their language skills. Bruno and Lola were happy that they could help the human learn, just like the parrot had helped them.

As the weeks went by, Bruno and Lola's English improved. They were able to communicate with humans and other dogs in English. They had made many new friends and had even discovered new parts of the city.

On their last day in London, Bruno and Lola went back to the park where they had met the squirrel on their first day. The squirrel was surprised to see how well they could speak English now.

Bruno and Lola said goodbye to their new friends and promised to come back one day. They knew that they would always have a special connection to London and to the English language.

And so, Bruno and Lola went back to Spain, feeling proud of all that they had learned. They continued to sing "The Wheels on the Bus" every day, remembering their adventure in London and the unique ways that they had learned English.

TEST YOURSELF

1. What made Bruno and Lola decide to go to London?
a) They wanted to learn French.
b) They heard London was the best place to learn English.
c) They wanted to meet new friends.

2. What did Bruno and Lola struggle with in their English class?
a) The other dogs were mean to them.
b) The teacher spoke too fast.
c) They had trouble sitting still.

3. What unique method did the parrot teach Bruno and Lola to help them learn English?
a) Reading books
b) Watching movies
c) Singing songs

4. What did Bruno and Lola teach the human who was studying Spanish?
a) English words
b) French words
c) Spanish words

5. How did Bruno and Lola feel when they went back to Spain?
a) Sad that they couldn't stay in London longer.
b) Proud of all they had learned.
c) Upset that they had to leave their new friends.

DISCUSSION -- SPEAK OR WRITE

1. What was your favorite unique method that Bruno and Lola used to learn English? Would you use that method to learn a new language?
2. Bruno and Lola made a lot of new friends during their adventure in London. Have you ever made a new friend by trying something new or learning something different?
3. The story shows that language-learning can happen outside of a classroom setting. Do you think it's important to try more unique and creative ways of teaching and learning languages? Why or why not?

Answers

1. b) They heard London was the best place to learn English.
2. b) The teacher spoke too fast.
3. c) Singing songs.
4. c) Spanish words.
5. b) Proud of all they had learned.

ONE SMALL STEP FOR A DOG

Luna was a tiny little terrier with a big heart and a lot of determination. Her biggest dream was to go to Mars. She had always been fascinated by space, and had spent countless hours staring up at the night sky, wondering what it would be like to explore the great unknown.

One day, Luna decided that she was going to make her dream a reality. She set her sights on NASA, the world's leading space agency, and began to work tirelessly to convince them that she was the perfect dog for the job.

At first, Luna didn't know where to begin. She had no idea how to get to NASA, or how to convince them that a little dog like her could handle the difficulties of space travel. But Luna was nothing if not resourceful, and she soon began to create a plan.

She started by studying everything she could find about NASA and space travel.

She read books and articles, watched documentaries, and even talked to some of the local astronomers in her town. Luna was determined to become an expert on all things space-related.

Next, Luna began to train herself for the challenges she would face in space. She started by building up her endurance, running for miles every day to improve her cardiovascular fitness. She also worked on her agility, practicing her jumps and leaps until she could clear obstacles with ease.

But Luna knew that physical fitness was only part of the equation. She also needed to prove to NASA that she was smart and capable, so she started studying math, science, and engineering. She spent hours each day working on puzzles and equations, determined to master the skills she would need for space travel.

As Luna worked hard to prepare herself for her journey to Mars, she also began to reach out to NASA. She wrote letters and emails, made phone calls, and even showed up at the agency's headquarters in person. Luna was nothing if not persistent, and she refused to take no for an answer.

Despite her best efforts, however, Luna kept getting the same response from NASA: dogs weren't allowed in space. The agency had strict rules about who could go on space missions, and Luna just didn't fit the bill.

But Luna wasn't about to give up. She kept working hard, training every day and studying every night. And finally, her persistence paid off.

One day, a team of NASA scientists came to visit Luna's town. They were there to give a talk on space travel, and Luna knew that this was her chance. She snuck into the auditorium where the scientists were speaking, and when the talk was over, she went to talk to them.

At first, the scientists were surprised to see a little dog talking to them. But Luna was charming and persuasive, and she managed to win them over with her enthusiasm and determination. She explained her dream of going to Mars, and why she believed that she was the perfect dog for the job.

To her amazement, the scientists were impressed. They had never seen a dog with such dedication and passion for space travel. They agreed that she could go on their next mission, and Luna was over the moon with excitement.

In the months that followed, Luna continued to work hard to prove herself to NASA. She trained harder than ever, and even started building her own spacesuit, using materials she found around her home. She was determined to show the world that a little dog like her could do big things.

Finally, the day of the mission arrived. Luna put on her spacesuit and climbed aboard the spacecraft, ready to blast off into the unknown. As the countdown began, Luna felt her heart beating faster than ever before. She was nervous, but she was also filled with excitement and anticipation.

And then, with a deafening roar, the spacecraft blasted off into space, leaving Earth far behind. Luna felt the g-forces pressing against her body as the spacecraft flew through the atmosphere and into the darkness of space. But despite the intense physical sensations, Luna couldn't help but feel a sense of awe and wonder at the

ONE SMALL STEP FOR A DOG

incredible journey she was embarking on.

For weeks, Luna and the other members of the mission traveled through space, conducting experiments and gathering data about Mars. Luna was amazed by the beauty and mystery of the red planet, and she felt privileged to be among the first to explore it.

But then, disaster struck. One day, the spacecraft was hit by a massive solar flare, and Luna's section of the ship was badly damaged. The other members of the mission were able to make it back to Earth safely, but Luna was stranded on Mars, alone and afraid.

At first, Luna felt hopeless. She was alone on an alien planet, with no way to communicate with Earth or get back home. But then, she remembered all of the hard work and training she had done to prepare for this mission.

She knew that she had the skills and the determination to survive, even in the face of such incredible adversity.

And so, Luna set to work. She scrounged for resources and built herself a makeshift shelter, using rocks and soil from the Martian surface. She gathered food and water, and she explored the planet, searching for any signs of life or help.

Days turned into weeks, and weeks turned into months. Luna's time on Mars was difficult and lonely, but she never gave up hope. And finally, after what felt like an eternity, a rescue mission arrived to bring her back to Earth.

When Luna returned home, she was hailed as a hero. Her determination and courage had captured the hearts of people all over the world, and her story became the stuff of legend. And Luna knew that she had accomplished something truly remarkable. She had shown the world that even a little dog could achieve big things as long as she had the courage and determination to pursue her dreams.

TEST YOURSELF

1. What is the name of the dog who dreams of going to Mars?
a) Luna
b) Pluto
c) Apollo

2. How does Luna convince NASA to consider her for a mission to Mars?
a) She shows up at their headquarters in person
b) She writes letters and emails
c) She talks to local astronomers
d) All of the above

3. Why does NASA initially reject Luna's application?
a) They don't believe dogs can handle space travel
b) They already have a full crew for the mission
c) Luna is too small to be of any use

4. What happens to Luna during the mission to Mars?
a) She is left behind on the planet after the rest of the crew returns to Earth
b) She gets lost on the planet and has to be rescued
c) She becomes ill and has to be evacuated back to Earth

4. How is Luna received when she returns to Earth?
a) She is ignored and forgotten
b) She is criticized for being too small to be useful on the mission
c) She is hailed as a hero

DISCUSSION -- SPEAK OR WRITE

1. Why is it important to work hard to achieve our goals?
2. What can we learn from Luna's experience about being brave and resourceful when faced with difficult situations?
3. Why do you think Luna was hailed as a hero when she returned to Earth? What can we learn from Luna's story about never giving up, even when things seem impossible?

Answers

1. a) Luna
2. d) All of the above
3. a) They don't believe dogs can handle space travel
4. a) She is left behind on the planet after the rest of the crew returns to Earth
5. c) She is hailed as a hero

THE COOLEST DOG IN TOWN

Bertie was a lovable dog who lived with his human family in a cozy little house. Bertie had always admired cats from afar, especially the ones in the neighborhood who were always grooming themselves and jumping around gracefully.

One day, Bertie decided he wanted to be a cat too. "I wish I could climb trees like they do and be as cool as they are," he thought to himself.

So, Bertie set out on a mission to become a cat. He spent his days watching the neighborhood cats, trying to learn their secrets.

One day, Bertie's human sister, Mia, caught him staring at the cats in the yard.

"What are you looking at, Bertie?" she asked.

"I'm trying to learn how to be a cat," Bertie replied.

Mia laughed. "You can't be a cat, Bertie. You're a dog!"

"But I want to be as cool as the cats," Bertie insisted.

Mia shook her head. "You're already cool just the way you are, Bertie. Dogs are awesome too!"

Bertie wasn't convinced, though. He continued to watch the cats and try to copy their behavior. He even tried climbing a tree, but his big paws kept getting stuck in the bark.

One day, Bertie saw a group of cats playing in a nearby alleyway. He couldn't resist joining in on the fun and ran towards them, barking excitedly.

The cats, however, were not impressed. They

hissed and swiped at Bertie with their sharp claws, making him walk back to his humans' house with his tail between his legs.

Feeling sad about his failed attempts to be a cat, Bertie confided in his best friend, the family's pet bird named Charlie.

"I just want to be as cool as the cats," Bertie sighed.

Charlie chirped sympathetically. "But Bertie, you're already cool! You can do so many things that cats can't do, like fetch and swim."

Bertie smiled at Charlie's words. He realized that he didn't have to be a cat to be cool. He could be a cool dog!

From that day on, Bertie stopped trying to be a cat and started embracing his inner dog.

He went on longer walks with his humans, chased after Frisbees in the park, and even learned some new tricks.

One day, while Bertie was out on his daily walk, he saw a group of cats playing in a nearby field. Bertie really wanted to join them, but he remembered Charlie's words and decided to just watch them instead.

As he watched the cats, Bertie noticed that one of them was having trouble catching a butterfly. Bertie knew he was an expert at catching things, so he decided to help.

Bertie trotted over to the cat and gently picked up the butterfly in his mouth. The cat looked surprised but grateful.

"Thanks, Bertie!" the cat said, nuzzling Bertie's nose.

Bertie felt a warmth in his heart. Maybe he didn't have to be a cat to make friends with them after all.

From that day on, Bertie started spending more time with the neighborhood cats. He would watch them play and sometimes even join in on their games of chase. The cats started to warm up to Bertie and even let him groom them, something they would never have done before.

From that day on, Bertie continued to spend time with the cats and even started teaching them some of his dog tricks. The cats were amazed at what he could do, and they were proud to have Bertie as their friend.

Bertie felt like he had finally found his place in the world. He didn't need to be a cool cat because he was already the coolest dog in town.

TEST YOURSELF

1. What was the name of the dog in the story?
a) Max
b) Bertie
c) Charlie

2. What did Bertie want to be in the beginning of the story?
a) A bird
b) A cat
c) A fish

3. Who helped Bertie realize that he didn't need to be a cat to be cool?
a) The neighborhood cats
b) His human sister, Mia
c) The family's pet bird, Charlie
d) His dog friends from the park

4. What game did Bertie play with the cats?
a) Frisbee
b) Tag
c) Chase

5. What lesson did Bertie learn in the end?
a) Being true to oneself is the key to happiness
b) Cats are cooler than dogs
c) Trying to be someone else is the way to make friends

DISCUSSION -- SPEAK OR WRITE

1. What do you think made Bertie change his mind about wanting to be a cat? Do you think it was a good decision? Why or why not?
2. Do you think it's important to be yourself, even if others might not like you? Why or why not?
3. Bertie learned that he didn't have to be a cat to be cool. What do you think makes someone or something cool? Do you think it's important to try to be cool, or is it better to just be yourself? Why?

Answers

1. b) Bertie
2. b) A cat
3. c) The family's pet bird, Charlie
4. c) Chase
5. a) Being true to oneself is the key to happiness

WOOFY'S WONDERFUL MEALS

Once upon a time, there was a cute little dog named Woofy who lived in a cozy little house with his loving owners, Mr. and Mrs. Jones. Woofy loved nothing more than snoozing in his basket and snacking on the occasional dog biscuit.

But one day, something strange happened. Woofy woke up feeling different. He had a sudden urge to cook! He jumped out of his basket, wagged his tail, and ran over to the kitchen.

As he approached the counter, Woofy's nose twitched at the smells of meat, vegetables, and spices. He decided to experiment and

cooked a tasty dish of beef and vegetables—with lots of gravy. He mixed it with some dog-friendly ingredients and took a bite. It was delicious!

Woofy decided to share his creation with his canine friends at the dog park. They loved it! Word quickly spread, and before Woofy knew it, dogs all over town were lining up to try his gourmet dog food.

Woofy knew he was onto something big, so he decided to start his own business. He named it "Woofy's Wonderful Meals" and began selling his food at the local farmer's market.

The first day, there was a long line of hungry dogs with their owners waiting for Woofy's meals. As they got to the front of the line, they were surprised to see a cute little dog in a chef's hat cooking away!

"Welcome to Woofy's Wonderful Meals!" Woofy barked. "What can I get for you and your furry friend?"

The dogs were amazed. They had never seen a dog chef before! Woofy cooked everything from salmon and sweet potato stew to chicken and rice curry. The dogs licked their bowls clean and wagged their tails in delight.

Woofy's business was an instant hit, and soon he had a team of doggy sous chefs helping him create his gourmet recipes. Woofy's Wonderful Meals became a global sensation, with dogs all over the world hoping for a taste.

Mr. and Mrs. Jones were overjoyed at their little dog's success. They watched as Woofy became a celebrity, appearing on TV talk shows and cooking competitions.

One day, as Woofy was cooking up a batch of his famous beef stew, he heard a knock at the door. It was a group of snooty cats, led by a Siamese named Mrs. Whiskers.

"We've heard about your little doggy business," Mrs. Whiskers sneered. "And we're here to tell you that cats are the true connoisseurs of fine dining. We demand that you cater to our sophisticated palates!"

Woofy was taken aback. He had never cooked for cats before! But he didn't want to disappoint his customers, so he decided to give it a try.

Woofy cooked a special batch of his beef stew, adding in some cat-friendly ingredients. Mrs. Whiskers and her group of cats gathered around the bowl, sniffing at it suspiciously.

"It smells acceptable," Mrs. Whiskers declared. "Let us try it."

The cats took a tentative bite, then another, and another. Before they knew it, they were licking their bowls clean and purring with pleasure.

"Simply divine!" Mrs. Whiskers exclaimed. "You have truly surpassed our expectations, Woofy. From now on, we shall be coming here every week."

Woofy was overjoyed. He had never imagined that he would be cooking for cats too! As word of his cat-friendly dishes spread, more and more felines began flocking to his stall at the farmer's market.

With his business booming, Woofy decided to open his own restaurant. He hired a team of talented chefs and waitstaff and opened the doors to Woofy's Wonderful Meals.

The restaurant was a huge success, with dogs and cats from all over the world visiting to sample Woofy's gourmet creations. Woofy was now a celebrity chef, appearing on cooking shows and being interviewed by the likes of Oprah Winfrey and Ellen DeGeneres.

But despite his fame, Woofy never forgot his humble beginnings. He still loved nothing more than snoozing in his basket and snacking on the occasional dog biscuit. And every day, he woke up feeling grateful for his amazing adventure as a dog chef.

TEST YOURSELF

1. What was the name of the cat in the story?
a) Max
b) Mrs. Whiskers
c) Woofy
d) Fido

2. What did Woofy feel like doing one day that was different from his usual routine?
a) Going for a walk
b) Watching TV
c) Cooking

3. What did Woofy name his gourmet dog food business?
a) Woofy's Wonderful Meals
b) Max's Mutts Meals
c) Spot's Specialties
d) Fido's Feast

4. Who came to Woofy's restaurant to try his food?
a) Dogs only
b) Cats only
c) Dogs and cats
d) Birds and fish

5. Where did Woofy sell his food?
a) At the farmer's market
b) Online
c) At the local shopping mall

DISCUSSION -- SPEAK OR WRITE

1. What was your favorite part of Woofy's story? What did you learn from Woofy about following your passions and dreams?
2. How important is eating healthy food to you?
3. Would you like to start up a small business? If so, what would it be?

Answers

1. 1. a) Mrs. Whiskers
2. 2. c) Cooking
3. 3. a) Woofy's Wonderful Meals
4. 4. c) Dogs and cats
5. 5. a) At the farmer's market

MUFFLE'S MARVELOUS MUSTACHE

Muffles was a friendly and fluffy dog who loved to play and go on adventures. One day, he woke up and discovered something very strange: he had grown a big, bushy mustache overnight!

Muffles was surprised and confused. He had never seen anything like it before. He ran to the mirror and stared at himself. "Woof woof!" he barked. He didn't recognize himself with his new mustache.

His owner Lily came in and saw Muffles staring at himself. "What's wrong, boy?" she asked.

Muffles barked and wagged his tail, trying to show her his new mustache. Lily looked at him and gasped.

"Oh my goodness, Muffles, you have a mustache!" she exclaimed.

Muffles barked again, as if to say, "I know!"

Lily called her friends over to see Muffles' new look. "You won't believe what happened to Muffles!" she told them.

When Lily's friends arrived, they were amazed by Muffles' mustache. They took pictures and laughed at him. Muffles didn't mind. He was happy to be the center of attention.

But as the day went on, Muffles started to feel different. He felt more confident and sophisticated with his new mustache. He even started to talk differently.

"Good day, madam," he said to Lily's friend. "Would you care for a cup of tea?"

Lily and her friends laughed. "Did Muffles just talk?" one of them asked.

Muffles barked, trying to tell them that he was still the same old dog, just with a new mustache.

As time went on, Muffles' mustache grew even bigger and bushier. He started to attract attention wherever he went. People would stop and take pictures of him, and other dogs would stare at him in amazement.

Muffles loved the attention, but he also started to feel a little bit uncomfortable. He didn't like being stared at all the time, and he didn't like being treated differently just because of his mustache.

One day, Muffles was walking in the park when he met an old dog named Rusty. Rusty was a wise old dog who had seen a lot in his life.

He looked at Muffles and said, "You know, Muffles, there's more to life than just looks. It's what's on the inside that really counts."

Muffles realized that he had become too focused on his appearance, and that it was more important to be a good and kind dog.

As time passed, Muffles' mustache grew even larger, and he started to feel uncomfortable with the extra attention it brought him. He realized that he didn't need to rely on his appearance to feel good about himself, and that being himself was enough.

From that day on, Muffles started to act differently. He didn't try to show off his mustache all the time, and he didn't care if people didn't pay attention to him anymore.

He just focused on being the same friendly and adventurous dog he had always been.

Over time, Muffles' mustache started to grow even bigger and bushier. But he didn't mind. He knew that his true value came from his personality and his actions, not from his appearance.

Eventually, Muffles' mustache became so big that he could hardly see over it. He knew it was time to trim it down. He went to the groomer and had it trimmed back to a more manageable size.

When Muffles returned to the park, the other dogs hardly recognized him. They asked him where his mustache had gone, and why he had trimmed it down.

Muffles just smiled and barked, "I'm still the same old Muffles, just with a smaller mustache."

The other dogs realized that Muffles was right. He was still the same friendly and adventurous dog they had always known and loved. And that was all that really mattered.

From then on, they treated Muffles just like they always had, with love and respect.

Muffles learned that true beauty comes from within, and that it's important to be true to oneself. From then on, Muffles lived a happy and fulfilling life, always staying true to himself and never forgetting what was really important.

TEST YOURSELF

1. What was Muffles' reaction when he saw his mustache for the first time?
a) He barked in excitement
b) He was confused and surprised
c) He felt scared and hid

2. What did Muffles start to feel after growing his mustache?
a) More confident and sophisticated
b) Scared and self-conscious
c) Indifferent and uninterested

3. How did the other dogs react to Muffles' mustache in the park?
a) They were impressed and amazed
b) They laughed and made fun of him
c) They ignored him and continued playing

4. What did Rusty tell Muffles when they met in the park?
a) Looks are the most important thing in life
b) Personality and actions matter more than appearance
c) Muffles should be ashamed of his mustache

5. How did Muffles' behavior change after meeting Rusty?
a) He became more arrogant and showy
b) He started to focus more on his appearance
c) He began to value his personality and actions more

DISCUSSION -- SPEAK OR WRITE

1. Have you ever tried a new hairstyle or piece of clothing and felt different or more confident? Why do you think that is? Can the way we look affect the way we feel?
2. Muffles realized that it's not your appearance that counts, but your actions and your personality. What do you think makes a person or animal truly special and valuable? Is it their appearance or something else?
3. Muffles learned to be true to himself and not worry about what others think. Have you ever felt like you had to change who you are or what you like because of other people's opinions? How did it make you feel, and what did you do about it?

Answers

1. b) He was confused and surprised
2. a) More confident and sophisticated
3. b) They laughed and made fun of him.
4. b) Personality and actions matter more than appearance.
5. c) He began to value his personality and actions more.

UNLEASHING THE PAST

Nelly was a little dog with a big heart. She loved playing with her toys and going for long walks with her owner, Lucy. But one day, something strange happened. Nelly found herself transported back in time, to a world she never knew existed.

The first dog Nelly met was Rin Tin Tin, the famous German Shepherd. Rin Tin Tin was a Hollywood superstar in the 1920s and 30s, starring in over 20 films. He was famous for his loyalty, intelligence, and bravery, and had become a household name around the world. Rin Tin Tin had even saved his owner's life

during World War I, becoming a symbol of hope and courage for many.

"Hello there," Rin Tin Tin said, wagging his tail at Nelly. "What brings you to this place?"

"I'm not sure," Nelly said, looking around in wonder. "One minute I was napping, and the next thing I knew, I was here."

"This is the Past Dog Park," Rin Tin Tin explained. "It's a magical place where dogs from all different times and places can come and play together. It seems like you belong here too."

Nelly smiled, feeling happy to have made a new friend. She spent the whole day playing with Rin Tin Tin, learning about his adventures and his life in Hollywood. She learned that Rin Tin Tin was much more than just a movie star - he was a symbol of hope and courage, a dog who had overcome incredible challenges to become one of the most beloved animals in history.

As the day drew to a close, Nelly said goodbye to Rin Tin Tin and went off to explore the rest of the park. She met Lassie, the brave Collie who had saved many people in her time. Lassie was famous for her intelligence and her ability to sense danger before anyone else. She had starred in movies, TV shows, and even comic books, becoming an icon for many.

"Hello, Nelly," Lassie said, wagging her tail. "I've heard a lot about you. What brings you to the Past Dog Park?"

"I'm not really sure," Nelly admitted. "I just ended up here somehow."

"Well, you're welcome to stay and play with us," Lassie said, smiling.

Nelly was thrilled. She spent the whole day playing with Lassie, learning about her many adventures and her incredible ability to sense danger. Lassie had saved countless lives over the years, becoming a true hero to many.

As the sun began to set, Nelly said goodbye to Lassie and went off to explore the rest of the park. She met Toto, the little Cairn Terrier who had become famous for his role in *The Wizard of Oz*. Toto was a small dog with a big personality, and he had captured the hearts of audiences around the world with his cute attitude and his loyalty to Dorothy.

"Hi, Nelly," Toto said, barking happily. "What brings you to this place?"

"I'm not really sure," Nelly said. "I just ended up here somehow."

"Well, you're welcome to stay and play with me," Toto said, wagging his tail. "Let me tell you about my adventures in Oz."

Nelly listened in amazement as Toto told her

all about his adventures with Dorothy and the other characters in Oz. She learned that Toto had played a crucial role in helping Dorothy find her way home, becoming a symbol of loyalty and friendship in the process.

As the day drew to a close, Nelly said goodbye to Toto and went off to explore the rest of the park. She met many other famous dogs along the way, from Gidget, the Chihuahua who had become famous for his role in Legally Blonde, to Beethoven, the lovable St. Bernard who had starred in his own series of movies.

Nelly had never felt so alive. She was learning so much about the incredible dogs who had come before her, and she felt proud to be a part of the same history.

As the day drew to a close, Nelly began to feel a sense of sadness. She didn't want to leave her new friends, but she knew that she had to go back to her own time.

"Goodbye, everyone," Nelly said, wagging her tail. "I had such a wonderful time here."

"Goodbye, Nelly," Rin Tin Tin said. "Remember, you're a part of dog history too."

Nelly smiled, feeling grateful for the incredible adventure she had just had. As she closed her eyes and drifted off to sleep, she knew that she would never forget this magical day.

She had met some of the most famous dogs in history, and she had learned that there was so much more to being a dog than just playing with toys and going for walks. Nelly felt proud to be a part of such a rich and diverse history, and she knew that she would carry this knowledge with her for the rest of her days.

TEST YOURSELF

1. What is the name of the main dog in the story?
a) Lucy
b) Toto
c) Rin Tin Tin
d) Nelly

2. What is the Past Dog Park?
a) A park where dogs from all different times and places can come and play together.
b) A park where only famous dogs are allowed.
c) A park where dogs can travel back in time.
d) A park where dogs can learn about history.

3. Who is Rin Tin Tin?
a) A little Cairn Terrier who starred in The Wizard of Oz.
b) A brave Collie who saved many people
c) A Hollywood superstar in the 1920s and 30s, starring in over 20 films.

4. What is Lassie famous for?
a) Her intelligence and her ability to sense danger.
b) Her loyalty, intelligence, and bravery.
c) Her spunky attitude and her loyalty to Dorothy.
d) Her role in Legally Blonde.

5. What does Nelly learn from her adventure at the Past Dog Park?
a) Dogs have played important roles throughout history.
b) There is so much more to being a dog than just playing with toys and going for walks.
c) She is a part of dog history too.
d) All of the above.

DISCUSSION -- SPEAK OR WRITE

1. If you could meet a famous dog from a long time ago, which one would you pick and why?
2. If you could go back in time, where would you go and what would you want to see?
3. Do you think it's important to learn about our history and where we came from? Why?

Answers

1. d) Nelly
2. a) A park where dogs from all different times and places can come and play together.
3. c) A Hollywood superstar in the 1920s and 30s, starring in over 20 films.
4. a) Her intelligence and her ability to sense danger.
5. d) All of the above.

MYSTIC: THE DOG WHO COULD SEE THE FUTURE

In the small town of Willow Creek, there lived a dog named Mystic. Mystic was no ordinary dog - she had a special gift. She could see into the future.

Mystic's human family, the Browns, were a kind and loving family who treated her like one of their own. They soon discovered Mystic's gift and began to rely on her for making important decisions.

One day, Mr. Brown was offered a new job in a big city. The family was excited about the opportunity, but Mystic had a vision that

something terrible would happen if they moved.

Mr. Brown was skeptical, but Mrs. Brown trusted Mystic's gift. She decided to do some research and found out that the city they were planning to move to had a high crime rate and was not safe for families.

Thanks to Mystic's vision, the Browns decided to stay in Willow Creek. As it turned out, a series of robberies occurred in the city they were planning to move to, and they were grateful to have avoided the danger.

The Browns soon realized the true power of Mystic's gift and began to seek her guidance for everything from job offers to buying a new car. Mystic's visions always proved to be accurate, and the family felt blessed to have her in their lives.

One day, Mystic had a vision of a fire in the nearby woods. She became restless and started to bark to alert the Browns. They immediately knew that they had to do something to prevent the fire from spreading.

The Browns followed Mystic to the woods

and discovered that a group of teenagers had started a campfire that had gotten out of control. Thanks to Mystic's warning, they were able to put out the fire before it caused any major damage.

Word quickly spread about Mystic's gift, and people from all over the town came to seek her guidance. Mystic became a beloved figure in Willow Creek, and the Browns were proud to share her gift with others.

One day, a young girl named Megan came to the Browns' house with a request. Her parents were going through a tough time, and she didn't know what to do. Mystic immediately sensed the girl's distress and began to focus on her.

Mystic closed her eyes and entered a trance-like state. She saw a vision of Megan's parents getting into a huge argument and breaking up. But she also saw a glimmer of hope - a way for them to work through their issues and come back together.

Mystic opened her eyes and let out a low growl. The Browns knew that this was a sign that Mystic had seen something important.

"Mystic, what did you see?" Mrs. Brown asked.

Mystic barked once, which meant, "there is hope."

The Browns gave Mystic's message to Megan, and she felt a sense of relief. She knew that there was still a chance for her parents to work things out.

With Mystic's guidance, Megan's parents were able to work through their issues and come back together. They were grateful to

Mystic and the Browns for helping them in their time of need.

Mystic continued to use her gift to help others, and she became a well-known figure not only in Willow Creek but throughout the entire region. People came from far and wide to seek her guidance and wisdom.

But even with all the attention and praise, Mystic remained humble and kind, always willing to lend a paw to those in need. She spent her days playing with the Browns, napping in the sun, and occasionally offering her gift to those who needed it most.

As Mystic grew older, her vision began to fade, but her love for her family and her community remained as strong as ever. She lived a long and happy life, surrounded by the love of those who had been touched by her gift.

When Mystic passed away, the Browns and the entire town of Willow Creek mourned her loss. But they also celebrated her life and the incredible impact she had on so many people.

To honor Mystic's memory, the Browns decided to create a park in her honor, a place where people could come to play, relax, and remember the special dog who had touched so many lives.

And so, Mystic's legacy continued to live on, not only in the park that bore her name but in the hearts of everyone who had been lucky enough to know her. She had been a true gift to her family and her community, and they would never forget the lessons she had taught them about love, compassion, and the incredible power of one small dog's gift.

TEST YOURSELF

1. What was Mystic's special gift?
a) She could talk
b) She could fly
c) She could see into the future
d) She could change colors

2. What did Mystic warn the Browns about when they were considering a move to a big city?
a) A natural disaster
b) A high crime rate
c) A job loss
d) A family conflict

3. What did Mystic's vision help the Browns prevent?
a) A robbery
b) A car accident
c) A big fire

4. What did the Browns decide to do to honor Mystic's memory?
a) They created a park in her name
b) They wrote a book about her life and gift
c) They sold T-shirts and other merchandise with her image
d) They created a mural of her on the side of their house

5. What did the Browns do to prevent the fire from spreading in the nearby woods?
a) They called the fire department
b) They used water buckets to put out the fire
c) They followed Mystic's guidance to find the source of the fire and put it out
d) They waited for the fire to die down on its own

DISCUSSION -- SPEAK OR WRITE

1. Mystic's gift allowed her to see into the future and help people in need. If you had a similar gift, how would you use it to help others? Would you use it to make personal decisions or to help others, or both?
2. Mystic's legacy lived on long after she was gone, and the Browns decided to create a park in her honor to celebrate her life. If you were to create a similar memorial for someone you loved, what kind of tribute would you create and why?
3. If you could have one special talent, what would it be and why?

ANSWERS

1. 1. c) She could see into the future
2. 2. b) A high crime rate
3. 3. c) A big fire
4. 4. a) They created a park in her name
5. 5. a) They called the fire department

MYSTIC: THE DOG WHO COULD SEE THE FUTURE

Great work! Why not check out our other books? Here is one you might like:

Available now in all major online bookstores.

Thanks for reading this book. We hope you've had a great time with it and improved your English!

As authors, we're always eager to hear what you think, so we'd love it if you could take a moment to leave a review. Your honest feedback helps us improve our writing and also helps other readers decide if this book is right for them. Plus, we'd just really appreciate it!

Visit us at
www.bellanovabooks.com
for more great books to continue your learning journey.

www.ingramcontent.com/pod-product-compliance
Lightning Source LLC
LaVergne TN
LVHW091047100526
838202LV00077B/3066